A Harvest of Pineapple Designs
Beautiful Tablecloth
(1) 120 cm in diameter. Instructions on page 76.

1

2

3

4

(2) 27 cm in diameter.   Instructions on page 75.
(3) 25 cm in diameter.   Instructions on page 78.
(4) 29 cm in diameter.   Instructions on page 79.

Pretty Doilies

Handsome Centerpieces

(5) 38 cm in diameter. Instructions on page 80.
(6) 33 cm in diameter. Instructions on page 81.

5

A Dainty Dozen—doilies crocheted with only 10g

Miniature Masterpieces

(7) 20 cm in diameter.   Instructions on page 82.   (8) 24 cm in diameter.   Instructions on page 83.
(9) 21.5 cm in diameter.   Instructions on page 84. (10) 20 cm in diameter.   Instructions on page 85.
(11) 23 cm in diameter.   Instructions on page 86. (12) 17 cm in diameter.   Instructions on page 87.

7		10	12
8	9	11	

Accent on Good Looks

(13) 24 cm in diameter. Instructions on page 88. (14) 17 cm × 17 cm. Instructions on page 89.
(15) 22 cm in diameter. Instructions on page 90. (16) 20 cm in diameter. Instructions on page 91.
(17) 19.5 cm in diameter. Instructions on page 92. (18) 20 cm in diameter. Instructions on page 12.

	14	16	18
13	15		17

18

You'll need: DMC crochet cotton No. 40. 10g white (5200).
Steel crochet hook: Crochet hook 0.9 mm.
Finished size: 20 cm in diameter
Instructions: Row 1: Make a loop at the end of thread. (2-dc, (include the beginning ch-3), ch-3) 8 times. Row 2: 2-sl st, ch-1 at the beginning, repeat (1-sc, ch-13, 1-sc, ch-1, sl st-picot with 3-ch, ch-1). Row 3: 5-sl st, repeat (7-dc, ch-5). Row 4: Repeat (5-dc cluster, ch-5, 1-sc, ch-11, 1-sc,

ch-5). Row 5: Repeat (1-sc, ch-5, (1-dc, ch-2) 3 times, 1-dc, ch-5). From Row 6, work increasing and decreasing dc and ch. On Row 17, work around with sl st-picot with 3-ch and finish.

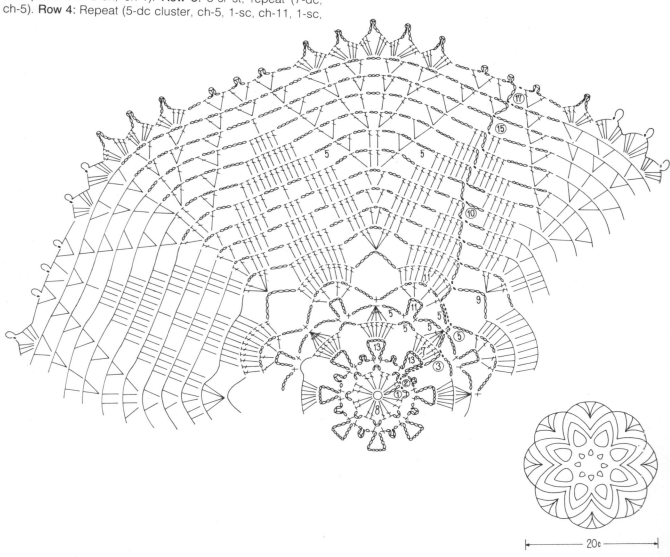

20c

12

You'll need: Crochet cotton No. 40. 10g gradation of green, light purple, yellow, blue, and pink. White cotton cloth, 13 cm×13 cm.

Steel crochet hook: Crochet hook 0.9 mm.

Finished size: 25 cm in diameter

Instructions: Cut cloth 13 cm in diameter. Fold the hem back 5 mm. Row 1: Work 2 sts in one point and make 280 sts. Row 2: Ch-3 at the beginning (work following row in same manner), 2-dc, and repeat ((ch-2, 1-dc) 9 times, ch-2, 3-dc, ch-3, 3-dc, (ch-3, 1-sc, ch-3, 1-dc) 4 times, ch-3, 1-sc, ch-3), 3-dc, ch-1, 1-hdc at the ends of row. Work filet st, increasing sts at 8 sides from Rows 3 to 10. Make 4-dc popcorn on Row 6. Work 3-dc puff on the last row and complete.

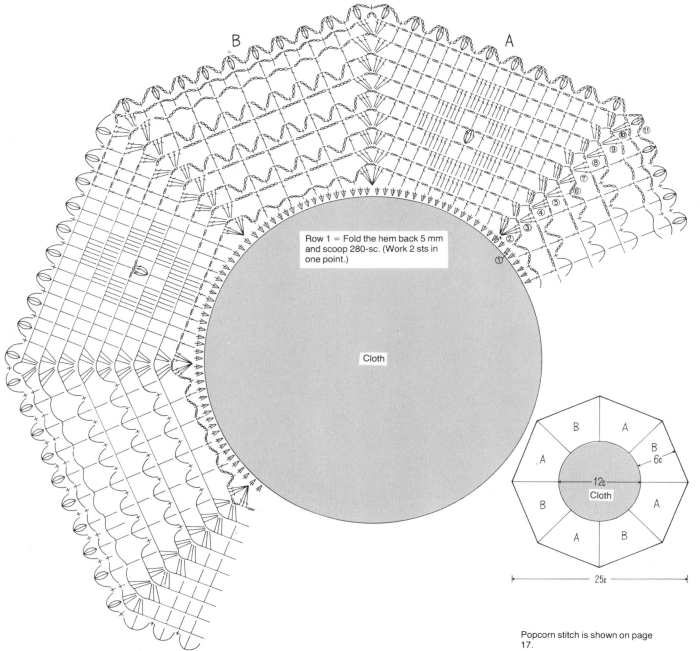

Row 1 = Fold the hem back 5 mm and scoop 280-sc. (Work 2 sts in one point.)

Cloth

Popcorn stitch is shown on page 17.

Perfect Coloring

(19) 25 cm in diameter.   Instructions on page 13.
(20) 24 cm in diameter.   Instructions on page 16.
(21) 21 cm in diameter.   Instructions on page 17.

Major and Minor Themes
Starbursts

(22) 21 cm in diameter.
(23) 39 cm in diameter.
Instructions on page 93.

23

22

You'll need: DMC crochet cotton No. 40. 10g light blue (800).

Steel crochet hook: Crochet hook 0.9 mm.

Finished size: 24 cm in diameter

Instructions: Ch-8, join with sl st to form ring. **Row 1:** Ch-3 (work following rows in same manner), 15-dc. **Row 2:** Repeat around with (1-dc, ch-2). **Row 3:** Repeat (1-sc, ch-9, 1-sc in same block of previous sc, ch-3) to make starfish shape. **Row 4:** Work (7-dc, ch-3, 7-dc) in 9-ch loop of previous row, 1-sc in ch-3 of previous row. Cut thread off. **Row 5:** Join thread in and start again. Work 2-dc cluster from Rows 9 to 13. Work around with sl st-picot with 3-ch on the last row.

Join thread in.
Cut thread off.

24c

You'll need: Crochet cotton No. 40. 10g gradation of light green, blue, and beige.

Steel crochet hook: Crochet hook 0.9 mm.

Finished size: 21 cm in diameter

Instructions: Row 1: Make a loop at the end of thread. Ch-3 at the beginning, 23-dc. **Row 2:** Repeat (2-dc cluster, ch-1). **Row 3:** Repeat (ch-3, 1-sc), ch-1, 1-hdc at the end. Increase ch on Rows 4 and 5. Continue in same manner,

except making shell st of 11-dc on Row 6. Work net st making small flower motifs at ▼ on Row 17. Finish, working net st of 8-ch on the last row.

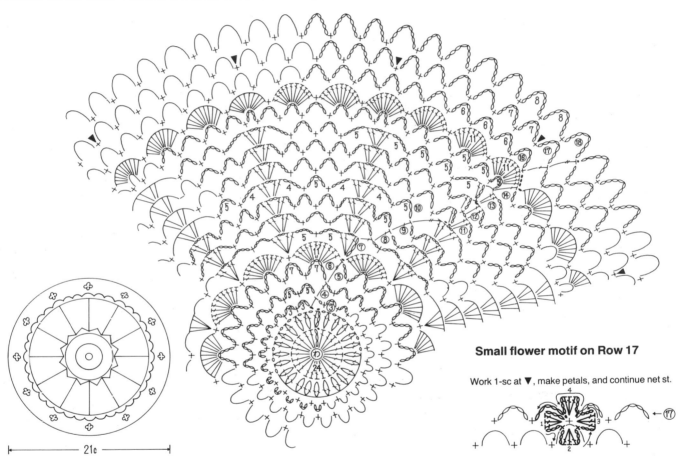

Small flower motif on Row 17

Work 1-sc at ▼, make petals, and continue net st.

─ 21c ─

4-double-crochet popcorn stitch.

① ② ③

24

(24) 20 cm in diameter.   Instructions on page 20.   (25) 28 cm in diameter.   Instructions on page 21.

18

25

Repeating a Good Idea

You'll need: DMC crochet cotton No. 40. 10g white (5200).

Steel crochet hook: Crochet hook 0.9 mm.

Finished size: 20 cm in diameter

Instructions: Make a loop at the end of thread. **Row 1:** Work 16-sc. **Row 2:** (1-sc, ch-5) 8 times. **Row 3:** Sl st in 2 sts of previous row and repeat (2-dc, ch-3, 2-dc). Work, increasing dc from Rows 4 to 8. Continue in same manner from Row 9. Work variation of sc on Row 14. Complete with sl st-picot with 3-ch between ch sts on the last row.

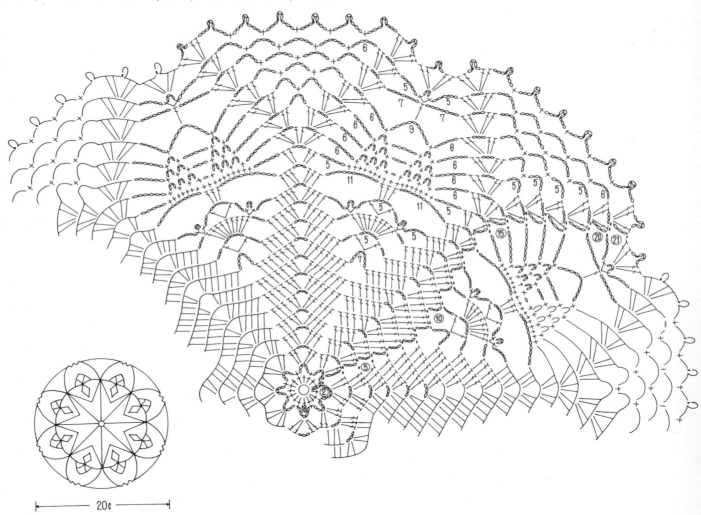

20c

25

You'll need: DMC crochet cotton No. 40. 20g white (5200).
Steel crochet hook: Crochet hook 0.9 mm.
Finished size: 28 cm in diameter

Instructions: Work same as for No. 24 through Row 20. Row 21: Sl st in 3 sts of previous row, and work as before. Complete with sl st-picot with 3-ch between ch on the last row.

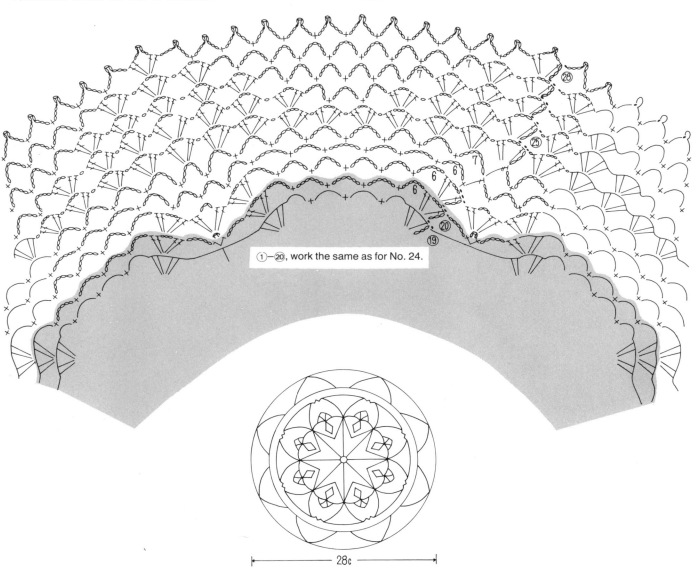

①—⑳, work the same as for No. 24.

28c

Hostess's Pride

(26) 126 cm×85 cm.   Instructions on page 24.

26

26

You'll need: DMC crochet cotton No. 20. 380g white (5200).

Steel crochet hook: Crochet hook 1.25 mm.

Finished size: 126 cm×85 cm

Instructions: Ch-265 and work filet st in center. The pattern is worked symmetrically from the center on both sides and up and down. Then make the outer part. Note that only the roses of the center are not symmetrical as shown. Make an edge on the last row, repeating (3-sc (4-sc from the second pattern), sl st-picot with 3-ch, 3-sc, ch-10, sl st in lst sc, ch-1, 7-sc, 3-sl st-picot, 7-sc, 5-sc in ch of previous row), the pattern of the corner being distinct in sc. Work referring to chart.

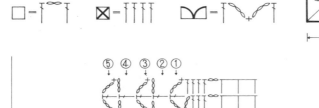

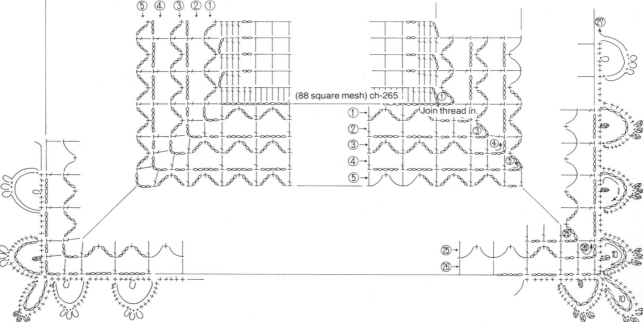

24

Center

79

70

60

50

40

30

20

10

5

1

88 square mesh ch-265

10

20

26

Multicolor Crochet
Pastel Harmonies

(27) 28.5 cm in diameter.   Instructions on page 94.
(28) 29 cm in diameter.   Instructions on page 28.

27

28

You'll need: DMC crochet cotton No. 40. 5g dark pink (3326), some pink (818), green (913), and blue (519).
Steel crochet hook: Crochet hook 1.0 mm.
Finished size: 29 cm in diameter
Instructions: Row 1: Make a loop with light brown (1-sc, ch-14, 4-sl st) 8 times. Use blue green on Rows 2 and 3. **Row 2:** Repeat (1-sc, ch-9). **Row 3:** Repeat (1-sc, ch-18, 8-sl st, ch-5). Use light brown from Rows 4 to 7, blue green on Row

8, light brown on Row 9, blue green from Rows 10 to 13, and light brown from Rows 14 to 19. Use blue green on Rows 20 and 21, pink on Row 22, green on Row 23, and pink on Rows 24 and 25, and finish.

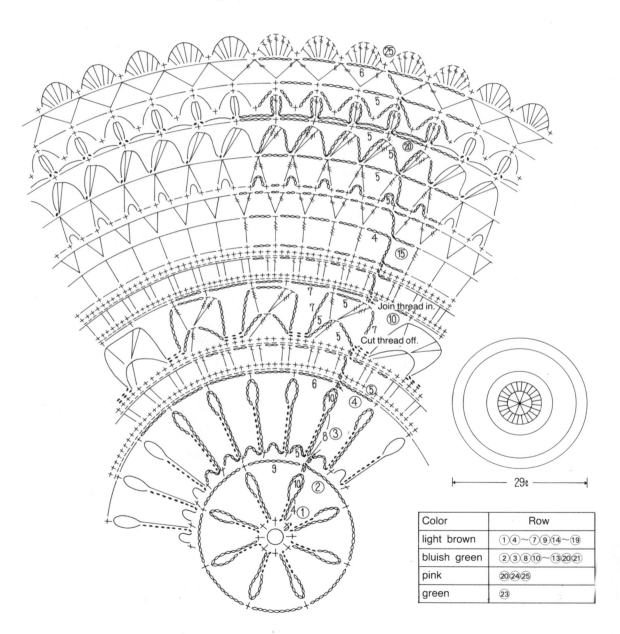

Color	Row
light brown	①④~⑦⑨⑭~⑲
bluish green	②③⑧⑩~⑬⑳㉑
pink	⑳㉔㉕
green	㉓

Shown on page 30

You'll need: DMC crochet cotton No. 40. 15g light purple (210), some light yellow (744), yellow green (954), blue (799), and pink (818).

Steel crochet hook: Crochet hook 0.9 mm.

Finished size: 27 cm in diameter

Instructions: Use light purple except for yellow green on Row 7, pink on Row 14, light yellow on Row 21, and blue on Row 28. **Row 1:** 8-sc in ring. **Row 2:** ch-3, 1-dc (ch-2, 2-dc in top of sc of previous row) 7 times, ch-2. Increase sts from Rows 3 to 6. Work variation of sc from Rows 7 to 9. Work in same manner changing colors until Row 31 and finish.

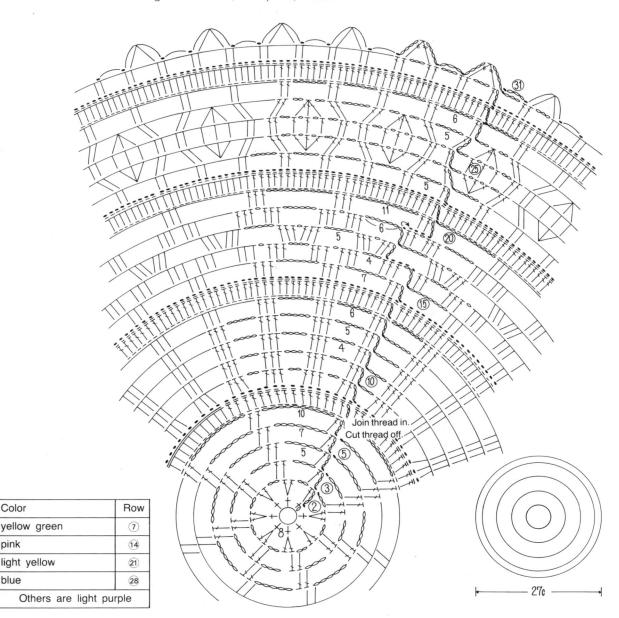

Join thread in.
Cut thread off.

Color	Row
yellow green	⑦
pink	⑭
light yellow	㉑
blue	㉘
Others are light purple	

27c

(29) 27 cm in diameter.   Instructions on page 29.
(30) 25.5 cm in diameter.   Instructions on page 32.

Spring Fling

30

You'll need: DMC crochet cotton No. 40. 10g each of light yellow (744) and light purple (554).
Steel crochet hook: Crochet hook 0.9 mm.
Finished size: 25.5 cm in diameter
Instructions: Row 1: Make a loop with light yellow, 9-sc. Work with light yellow and light purple alternately from Rows 2 to 11. **Row 2:** Ch-3 at the beginning, (ch-2, 1-dc) 8 times, ch-2 and join. **Row 3:** Repeat (1-sc, ch-3). Work in same manner increasing sts until Row 11. Use light purple on Rows 12 to 16. Work with light yellow and light purple alternately from Rows 17 to 22. **Row 23–28:** Use light purple. Work with light yellow on Row 29, light purple on Row 30, and light yellow on Rows 31 and 32. Break off.

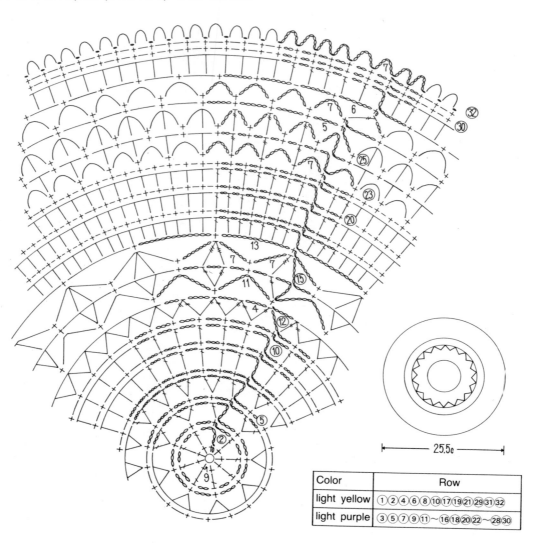

|←————— 25.5c —————→|

Color	Row
light yellow	①②④⑥⑧⑩⑰⑲㉑㉙㉜
light purple	③⑤⑦⑨⑪～⑯⑱⑳㉒～㉘㉚

You'll need: DMC crochet cotton No. 40. Some cream (745), pale green (952), pink (818), orange (742), green (913), blue (798), dark blue (823), red (666), light brown (437), and white (5200).
Steel crochet hook: Crochet hook 0.9 mm.
Finished size: 31 cm in diameter
Instructions: Work, changing colors in accordance with color chart. **Row 1:** Make a loop ch-1 at the beginning (work following row in same manner), 8-sc. **Row 2:** 2-sc in each sc

to make 16 sts. Work sc from Rows 3 to 5. **Row 6:** Repeat (1-tr, ch-2). **Rows 7 and 8:** Work sc. (Increase sts as shown.) Work Rows 9 to 20 and Rows 27 to 42 the same as Rows 6, 7, and 8. Work net st from Rows 21 to 26, sc and ch on Row 43, and repeat (5-ch net st, 1-sc, ch-1, 1-sc) on Row 44. Work sc on the last row to complete.

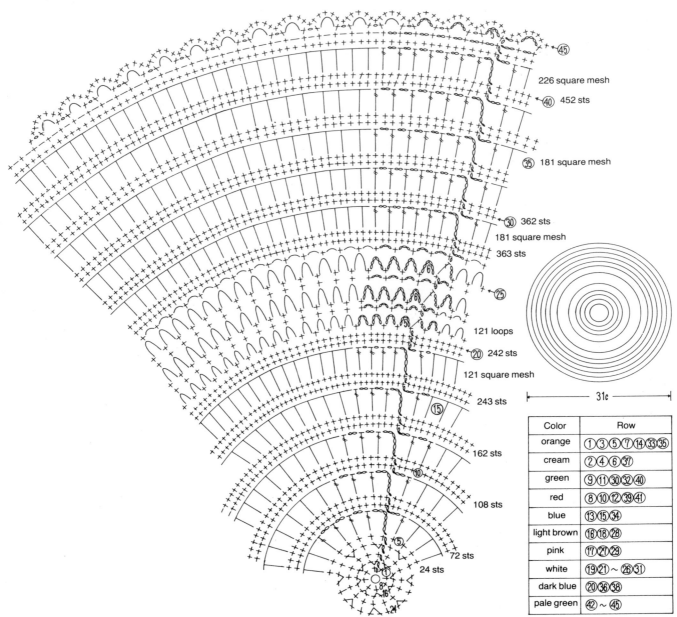

226 square mesh
452 sts
181 square mesh
362 sts
181 square mesh
363 sts
121 loops
242 sts
121 square mesh
243 sts
162 sts
108 sts
72 sts
24 sts

├─ 31c ─┤

Color	Row
orange	①③⑤⑦⑭㉝㉟
cream	②④⑥㊲
green	⑨⑪㉚㉜㊱
red	⑧⑩⑫㊴㊶
blue	⑬⑮㉞
light brown	⑯⑱㉘
pink	⑰㉗㉙
white	⑲㉑～㉖㉛
dark blue	⑳㊱㊳
pale green	㊷～㊺

Fiesta Motif

(31) 31 cm in diameter.   Instructions on page 33.   (32) 27 cm in diameter.   Instructions on page 95.

31

32

33

You'll need: DMC crochet cotton No. 40. 300g white (5200).
Steel crochet hook: Crochet hook 0.9 mm.
Finished size: 103 cm in diameter
Instructions: Row 1: Ch-3 at the beginning, (ch-1, 1-dc) 17 times in ring, sl st in 3rd st of beginning ch. Row 2: Repeat (ch-2, 1-dc). Row 3: 2-dc in ch-2 and 1-dc in dc of previous row to make 54 sts. Row 4: Repeat (ch-2, skip 1-dc. 1-dc in dc of previous row). Rows 5 and 6: Work same as for Rows 3 and 4. On Row 7, in accordance with the chart, work 3-ch picot between 2-dc in dc to make corners. Form 10 sections. Work in the same way from Row 8 to Row 116, increasing sts at the corner referring to chart.

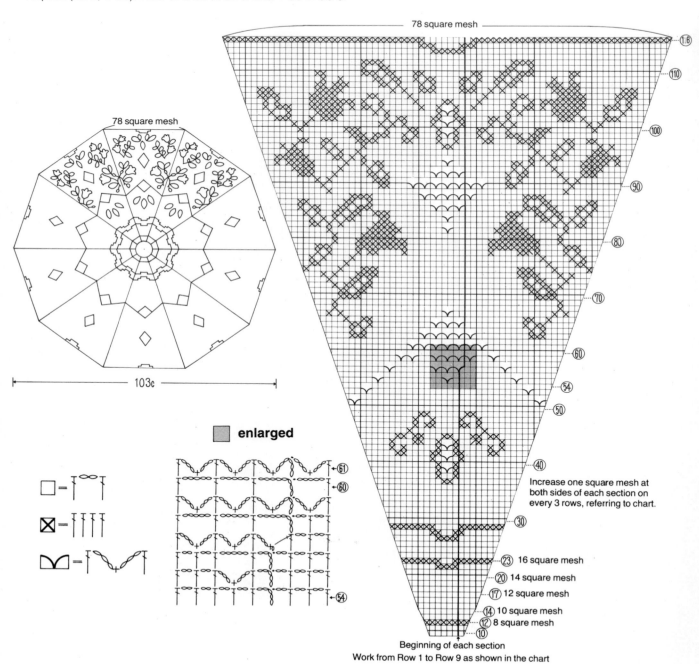

78 square mesh

103c

enlarged

Increase one square mesh at both sides of each section on every 3 rows, referring to chart.

16 square mesh
14 square mesh
12 square mesh
10 square mesh
8 square mesh
Beginning of each section
Work from Row 1 to Row 9 as shown in the chart

36

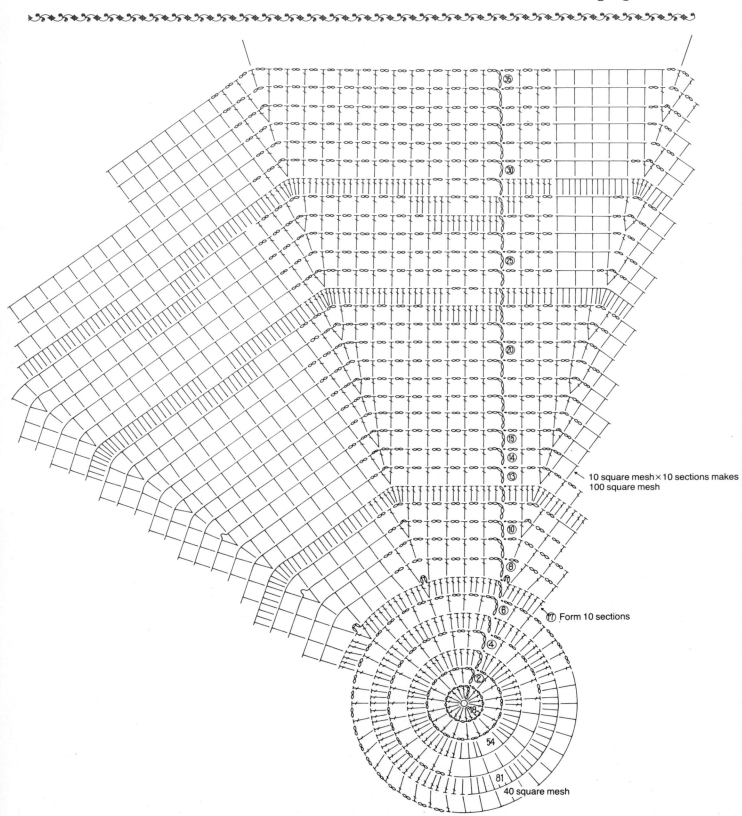

10 square mesh × 10 sections makes
100 square mesh

⑰ Form 10 sections

54

81

40 square mesh

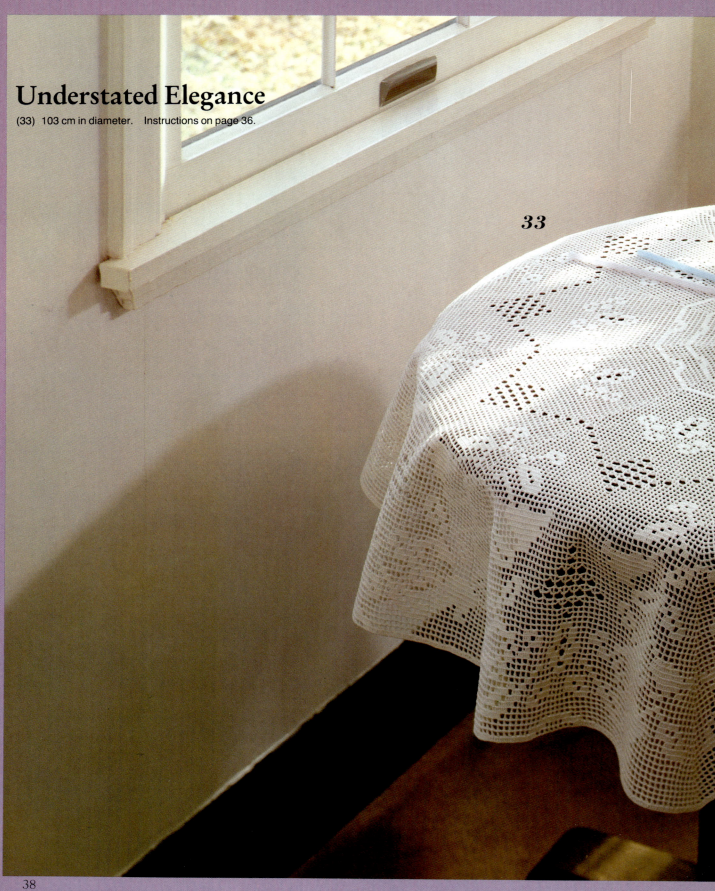

Understated Elegance

(33) 103 cm in diameter.   Instructions on page 36.

33

34

Shown on page 42

You'll need: DMC crochet cotton No. 30. 30g white (5200).
Steel crochet hook: Crochet hook 1.25 mm.
Finished size: 26 cm in diameter
Instructions: Ch-8, join with sl st to form ring. **Row 1:** Ch-3 at the beginning, 23-dc. **Row 2:** Repeat (3-dc, ch-3). **Row 3:** Work ch-5 between 3-dc. Work in accordance with chart from Row 4. Work 3-dc puff from Row 9. Complete the last row with sl st-picot with 5-ch.

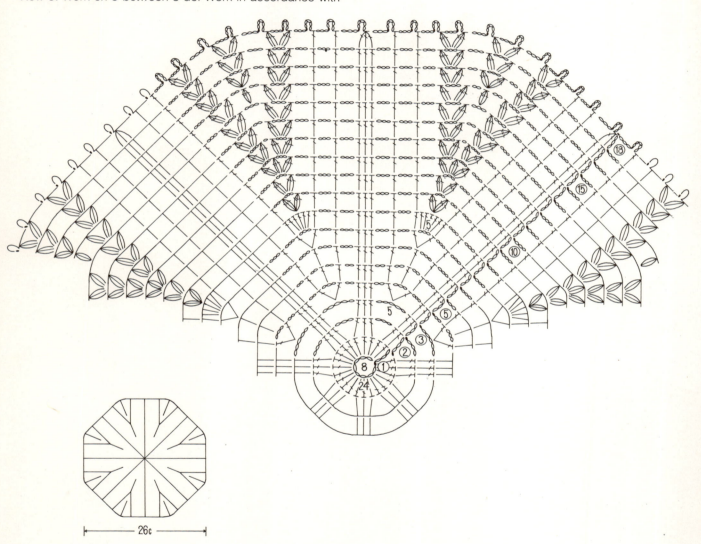

26c

35

You'll need: DMC crochet cotton No. 40. 15g white (5200).
Steel crochet hook: Crochet hook 0.9 mm.
Finished size: 25 cm in diameter
Instructions: Make a loop with the end of the thread.
Row 1: (3-tr puff (work ch-4 at the beginning), ch-4) 6 times.

Row 2: Repeat (ch-5, 1-sc), ch-1, 1-dc at the end. **Row 3:** Repeat (2-tr, ch-2). Continue working with tr and ch from Row 4 and work 3-tr puff from Rows 13 to 16. Complete the last row with ch-8, 2-tr cluster, and puff. (Note the points to scoop sts.)

25c

Doilies à la carte
Variations on a Theme

(34) 26 cm in diameter. Instructions on page 40.
(35) 25 cm in diameter. Instructions on page 41.
(36) 30 cm in diameter. Instructions on page 44.

42

You'll need: DMC crochet cotton No. 40. 30g white (5200).

Steel crochet hook: Crochet hook 0.9 mm.

Finished size: 30 cm in diameter

Instructions: Row 1: Make a loop. Repeat (3-dc (include the beginning ch-3), ch-1). **Row 2:** 3-sl st, repeat (3-dc, ch-3). **Row 3:** Work around with (5-dc, ch-5). **Row 4:** Repeat (7-dc, ch-3, 1-sc, ch-3). **Row 5:** Repeat (9-dc, ch-3, 1-sc, ch-3, 1-sc, ch-3), 1-sc, 1-hdc at the end of row. From Row 6, continue in same manner.

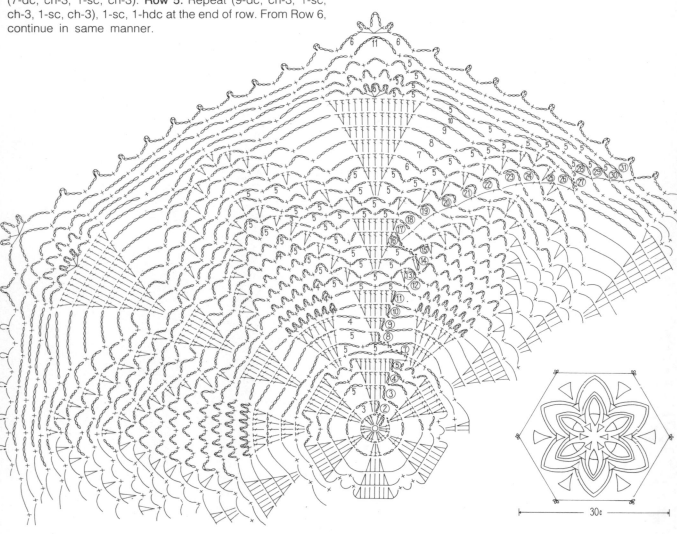

30c

37

You'll need: DMC crochet cotton No. 30. 45g white (5200).
Steel crochet hook: Crochet hook 1.5 mm.
Finished size: 35 cm in diameter
Instructions: Start from the center motif. Work 24 rows of A-braid and form a circle. Then join the center part with ch-1, 1-dc, and work 48 rows of A-braid, joining with the center motif, and form a circle. Join 8 pieces of motif the same as the center one. Work 128 rows of A-braid, joining them with 8

motifs to make the outer circle. Work ch-3, 1-dc (ch-3, sl st, ch-3, 4-dc) 2 times, ch-3, sl st, ch-3, 2-dc to make triangular pieces. In accordance with the B-braid chart, make the outer zigzag pattern. Be sure to draw 2 loops at a time from outer circle only once.

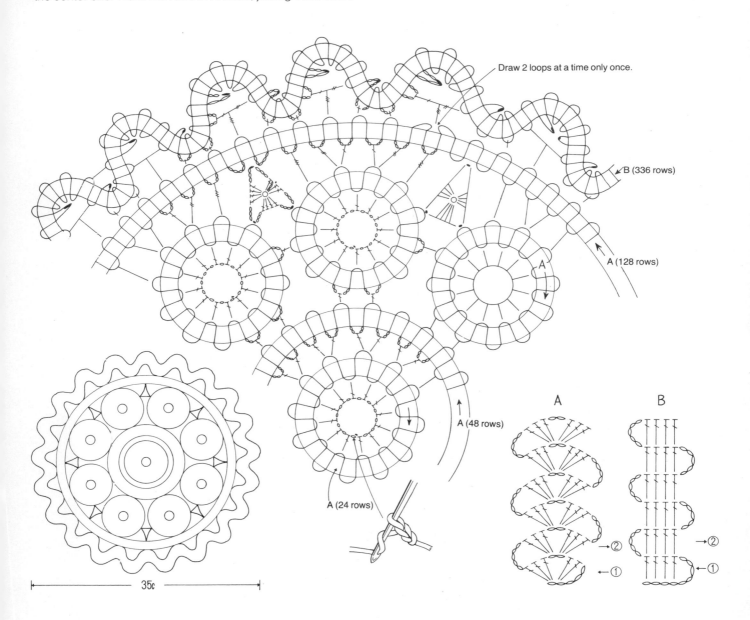

Draw 2 loops at a time only once.

B (336 rows)

A (128 rows)

A

A (48 rows)

A (24 rows)

35c

A   B

→②
←①

Classic Simplicity

(37) 35 cm in diameter.　Instructions on page 45.　　(38) 25 cm×25 cm.　　Instructions on page 48.

You'll need: DMC crochet cotton No. 30. 20g white (5200). DMC crochet cotton No. 40. 10g white (5200).
Steel crochet hooks: Crochet hooks 1.25 mm, 0.9 mm.
Finished size: 25 cm×25 cm
Instructions: Use 1.25 mm hook for crochet cotton No. 30 and 0.9 mm hook for crochet cotton No. 40. **Cord:** Make 8 cords 29 cm long with cotton No. 30, referring to chart and step F. Use cotton No. 40 for making motifs. **A=** Insert hook in loop. **Row 1:** (1-dc (include the beginning ch-3), ch-3) 8 times. **Row 2:** Repeat (1-sc, ch-2, 3-dc, ch-2, 1-sc). **Row 3:**

Work (ch-5, sl st between 2-sc of previous row) around. **Row 4:** Work the same as Row 2. **Row 5:** Repeat (ch-5, sl st in sc of previous row, ch-5, sl st). **Row 6:** Work 6-ch net st. **B=** Work as for A-motif until Row 4. Work the same from Row 5 to Row 7. On Rows 8 and 9, work net st joining to A-motif with sl st at three points of both sides. (Complete the center B-motif separately.) **C=** Work Row 7 on A-motif. **Finishing:** Arrange cords and motifs as shown in chart and sew from the back side with sewing cotton.

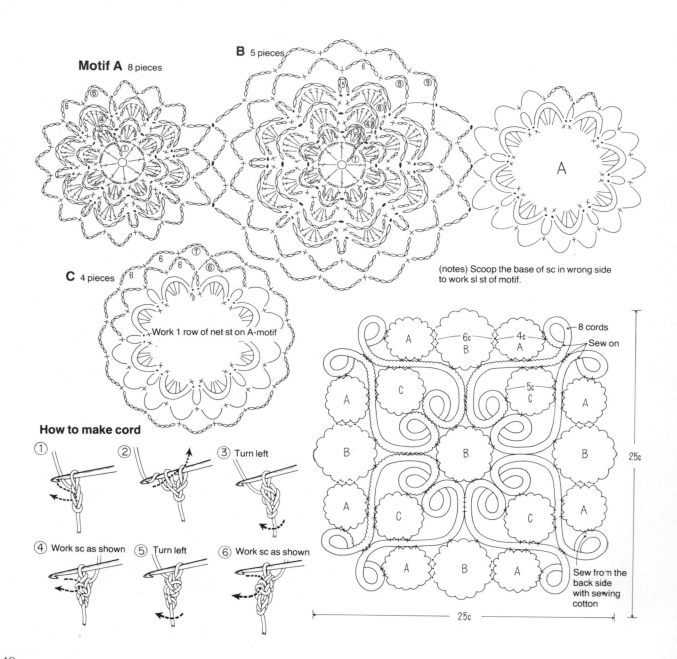

Motif A 8 pieces

B 5 pieces

C 4 pieces

Work 1 row of net st on A-motif

(notes) Scoop the base of sc in wrong side to work sl st of motif.

How to make cord

① ② ③ Turn left
④ Work sc as shown ⑤ Turn left ⑥ Work sc as shown

8 cords
Sew on
6c 4c
B
A
5c
C
A C A
B
B B
A C A
Sew from the back side with sewing cotton
A B A
25c
25c

You'll need: DMC crochet cotton No. 30. 25g white (5200).
Steel crochet hook: Crochet hook 1.25 mm.
Finished size: 28.5 cm in diameter
Instructions: Ch-7, join with sl st to form ring. **Row 1:** 8-sc. **Row 2:** Ch-3 at the beginning, (ch-3, 1-dc) 7 times,

ch-3, sl st in 3rd st of beginning ch. Work referring to chart from Row 3. On Row 22, repeat (7-dc, sl st-picot with 4-ch, 6-dc, 1-sc).

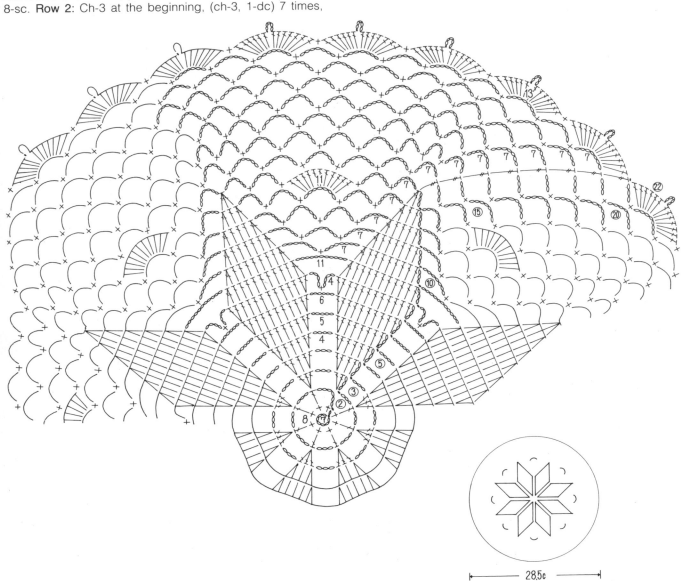

28,5c

Mostly Modern

(39) 28.5 cm in diameter. Instructions on page 49. (40) 30 cm in diameter. Instructions on page 52.

You'll need: DMC crochet cotton No. 40. 20g white (5200).
Steel crochet hook: Crochet hook 0.9 mm.
Finished size: 30 cm in diameter
Instructions: Row 1: 32-tr (include the beginning ch-3).
Row 2: Work (1-tr, ch-2) around. Row 3: Ch-1, repeat (1-sc, ch-7), ch-2, 1-tr at the end. Row 4: Work (ch-4, sl st-picot with 4-ch, ch-3, 1-sc) around. Row 5: Repeat (1-tr, ch-8).

Row 6: Repeat (6-sc, sl st-picot with 4-ch, 6-sc). Work 3-tr puff, ch, tr from Row 7 to 19. On Row 20, work ch and tr. Complete the last row with sl st-picot with 4-ch between hdc and ch.

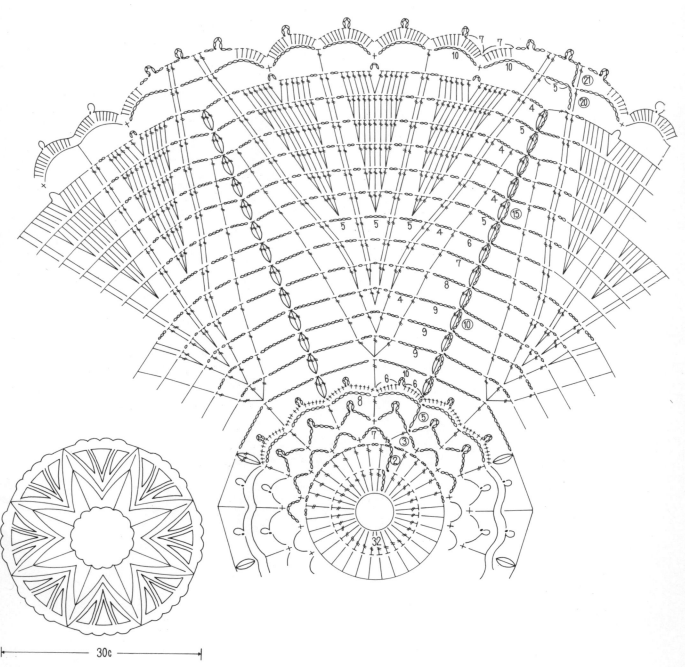

30c

You'll need: DMC crochet cotton No. 20. 40g beige (960).
Steel crochet hook: Crochet hook 1.5 mm.
Finished size: 34 cm in diameter
Instructions: Row 1: Ch-3 at the beginning, (ch-2, 1-dc) 7 times, ch-2 to form ring. Row 2: Work same, increasing ch.

Row 3: 5-dc, ch-3. Work increasing sts as shown from Row 4. Rows 17–20: Work around with sl st-picot with 3-ch between ch.

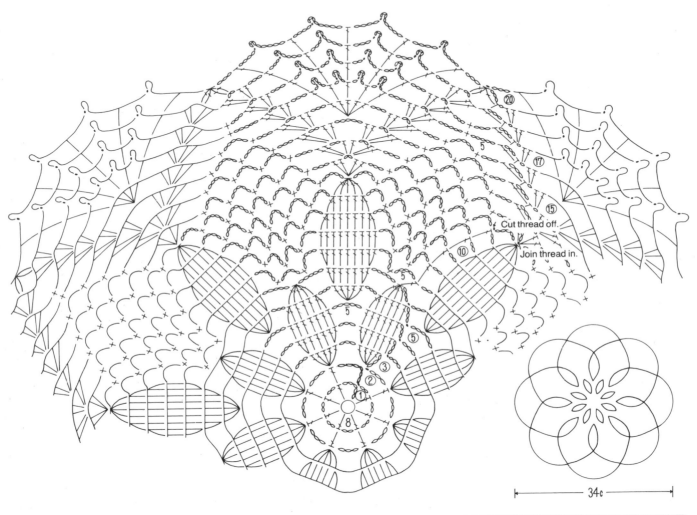

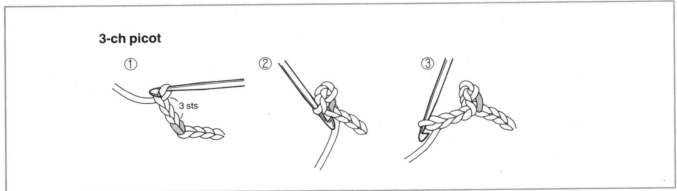

3-ch picot

41

Memories of Old Lace

(41) 34 cm in diameter.   Instructions on page 53.
(42) 27.5 cm in diameter.   Instructions on page 56.

42

You'll need: DMC crochet cotton No. 20. 25g beige (960).
Steel crochet hook: Crochet hook 1.5 mm.
Finished size: 27.5 cm in diameter
Instructions: Row 1: Make a loop, 12-sc. Row 2: Ch-3 repeat (ch-2, 1-dc). Row 3: Ch-11, back with dc. Repeat (sl st in the top of dc, ch-10, skip 6-dc, 1-dc, ch-1, 1-dc, ch-1, dc-1, ch-5, 1-dc in the top of dc of previous strip, ch-2, 1-dc, ch-2, 11-dc). Work back 7 sts with sl st after finishing 12 strips, ch-3, sl st, ch-1, 1-dc, ch-1, 1-dc, ch-5, 1-dc in the top of dc of previous strip, ch-2, 1-dc, ch-2, sl st at the end and cut thread off. Join thread in and continue to work after Row 4.

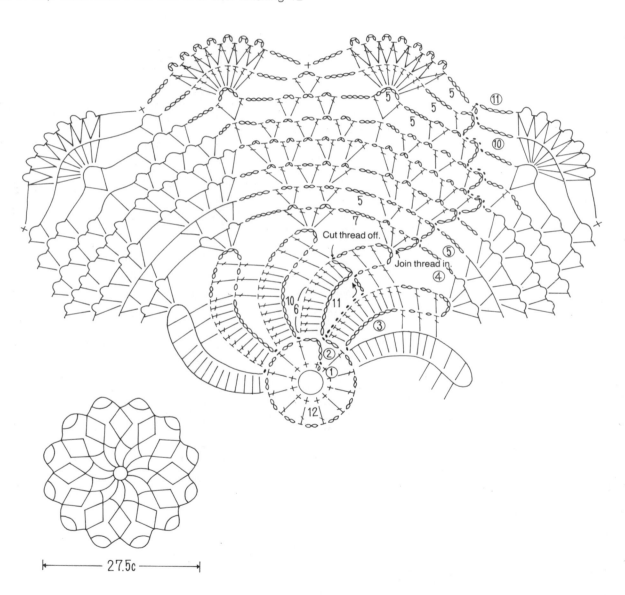

27.5c

You'll need: DMC crochet cotton No. 30. 60g white (5200).

Steel crochet hook: Crochet hook 1.5 mm.

Finished size: 42 cm×29 cm

Instructions: Row 1: Ch-3 at the beginning 3-dc, repeat (ch-2, 4-dc). Row 2: Ch-3, repeat (ch-2, 1-dc). Work filet st in same manner from Row 3. After finishing Row 45, continue to work edging repeating (ch-2, 4-dc (pick up sts from ch of square mesh)), 1-dc, ch-3, 3-dc in the base of dc. Complete with 4-dc at the end.

Fabulous Filet Work

Tablecloth: Free-wheeling Design

(43) 88 cm in diameter.   Instructions on page 60.

43

43

You'll need: DMC crochet cotton No. 30. 320g white (5200).
Steel crochet hook: Crochet hook 1.5 mm.
Finished size: 88 cm in diameter
Instructions: Make ch-190. **Row 1:** Ch-3 at the beginning, repeat (ch-2, 1-dc). **Row 2:** Ch-8 (include increasing 3 sts, beginning 3 sts and ch-2), 1-dc in each st of previous row. At end of row, work ch-2, 1-dtr in 3rd st of beginning ch of Row 1. From Row 3, work same as for Row 2, increasing sts of both sides. Work, decreasing sts in same manner. After completing 151 rows, continue to work 3 rows with (ch-5, 1-sc) and 1 row with (ch-2, sl st-picot, ch-2, 1-sc) for edging.

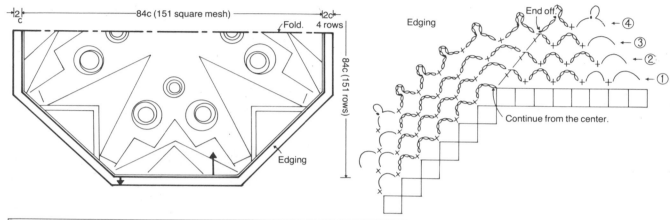

84c (151 square mesh) — Fold. 4 rows — 84c (151 rows) — Edging

Edging — End off. — Continue from the center.

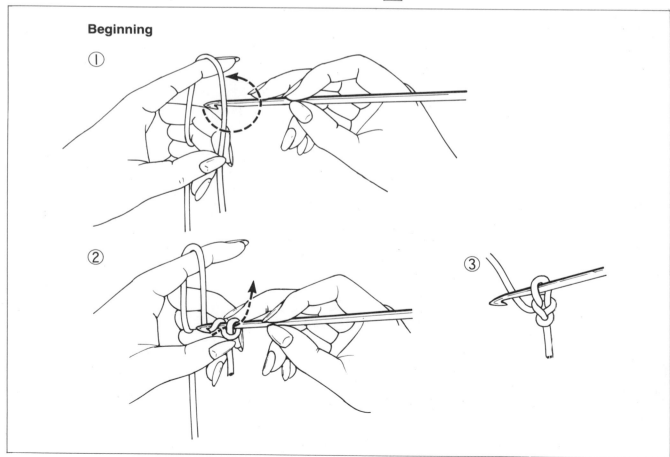

Beginning

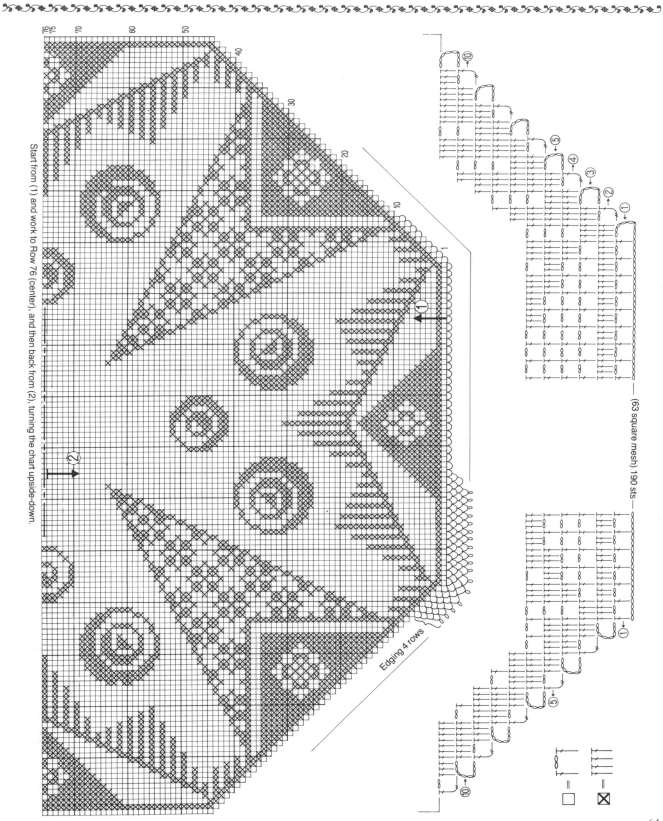

Start from (1) and work to Row 76 (center), and then back from (2), turning the chart upside-down.

(63 square mesh) 190 sts

Edging 4 rows

61

44

(44) 42 cm×29 cm.　　Instructions on page 57.
(45) 35 cm×29 cm.　　Instructions on page 64.
Duet in Circle and Line

45

You'll need: DMC crochet cotton No. 30. 50g white (5200).

Steel crochet hook: Crochet hook 1.5 mm.

Finished size: 35 cm×29 cm

Instructions: Ch-106. **Row 1:** Work dc. **Row 2:** (Increase 1 block.) Increase ch-3 and ch-3 at the beginning, 2-dc. Work following chart and 3-tr at the end of row to make corner. **Rows 3–8:** Work as for Row 2 increasing sts. **Row 13:** Decrease, working sl st at the beginning and remaining sts at the end. Hereafter work in same manner until Row 59.

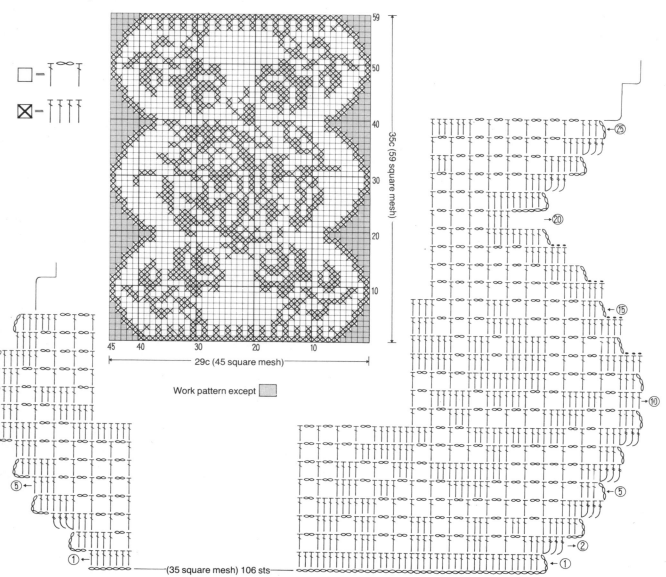

□ = ⊤⊤

⊠ = ⊤⊤⊤⊤

Work pattern except ▨

59
50
40
30
20
10

35c (59 square mesh)

45 40 30 20 10

29c (45 square mesh)

← 25
← 20
← 15
← 10
← 5
← 2
← 1

← 5
← 1

(35 square mesh) 106 sts

You'll need: DMC crochet cotton No. 30. 60g white (5200).
Steel crochet hook: Crochet hook 1.25 mm.
Finished size: 47 cm×30 cm
Instructions: Work 6 rows of left side first. Make ch-52. Row 2: Work 3-tr in base of the last dc. Start with ch-52 for right side and join both sides from Row 7. Continue working to Row 69 as shown, and work separately again from Row 70 and complete.

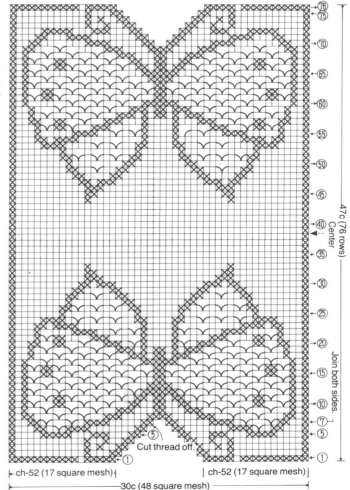

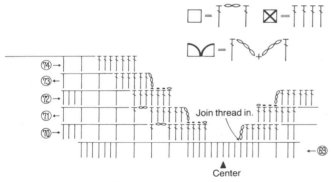

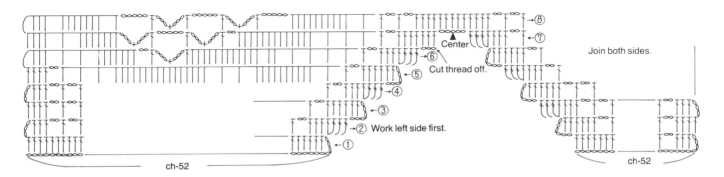

Stunning Statements

(46) 47 cm×30 cm.   Instructions on page 65.   (47) 58 cm×30 cm.   Instructions on page 68.

47

You'll need: DMC crochet cotton No. 30. 50g white (5200).

Steel crochet hook: Crochet hook 1.25 mm.

Finished size: 58 cm×30 cm

Instructions: Ch-4, in accordance with chart of the beginning, work increasing one block at both sides of every row. Work without any increase or decrease of sts from Rows 22 to 68, but the pattern is arranged symmetrically centering on Row 45. From Row 69, work decreasing one block at both sides of every row.

Valley enlarged

Beginning

4 sts

$\square$ =

$\boxtimes$ =

58c (89 rows)

Center

30c (43 square mesh)

You'll need: DMC crochet cotton No. 20. 70g beige (960).
Steel crochet hook: Crochet hook 1.5 mm.
Finished size: 66 cm in diameter
Instructions: Ch-12, join with sl st to form ring. **Row 1:** Ch-1 at the beginning, 21 sc. **Row 2:** Repeat (1-sc, ch-20), ch-10, octuple [eightfold] tr at the end. From Rows 3 to 11, work ch and sc referring to chart. On Row 12, work around with sc. **Row 13:** Repeat (ch-10, octuple tr, septuple tr, sextuple tr, ch-5, sextuple tr, septuple tr, octuple tr, ch-10,

1-sc). **Row 14:** Work around with (ch-40, 1-sc) as shown and cut thread. **Row 15:** Join thread, sc and ch until Row 25. Work sc on Row 26. **Row 27:** Repeat (1-sc, ch-3 (triple tr, ch-3) 2 times). **Row 28:** 6-tr popcorn. Work net st on Rows 29 to 31.

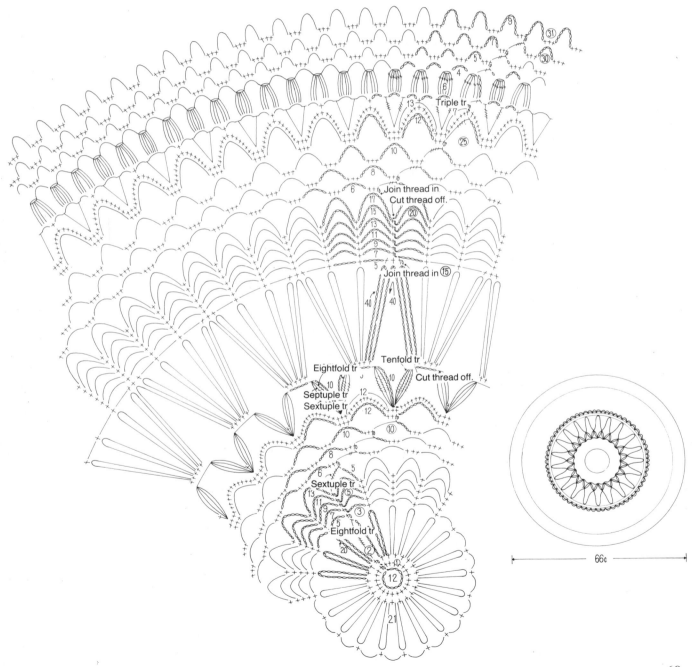

48

Quick Ways to Good Design

(48) 66 cm in diameter.   Instructions on page 69.
(49) 51 cm in diameter.   Instructions on page 72.

49

49

You'll need: DMC crochet cotton No. 20. 50g light cream (745).

Steel crochet hook: Crochet hook 1.5 mm.

Finished size: 51 cm in diameter

Instructions: Ch-7, join with sl st to form ring. Row 1: Ch-5, (ch-2, 1-dtr) 15 times, ch-2, sl st in 5th st of ch. Row 2: Sl st, ch-3 work around with (ch-5, 2-dc cluster (note the point to pick up)). **How to work A:** Ch-9, continue ch-7 for net st, (2-dc, ch-2) 2 times, 1-dc. Then, join with the center motif as shown on page 90. Join with sc at the end. On Row 3, begin from net st, repeat 1-sc, ch-6. Row 4: Work ch-8 (work sextuple tr from the 2nd petal), quintuple tr, triple tr, 1-dtr, 1-tr, 1-dc, and draw the top of every st, ch-7) around. Rows 5–10: Work referring to chart. **How to work B:** Work same as A. Rows 11–12: Work in same manner as for Rows 3 and 4. Rows 13–15: Work referring to chart.

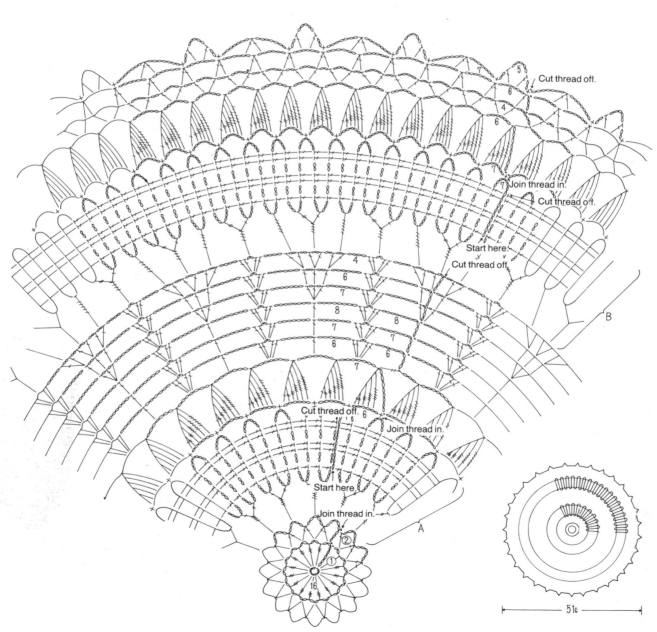

72

50

You'll need: DMC crochet cotton No. 30. 230g white (5200).
Steel crochet hook: Crochet hook 1.25 mm.
Finished size: 90 cm in diameter
Instructions: Row 1: Ch-3 in loop, 2-dc, (ch-2, 3-dc) 5 times, 1-hdc in 3rd st of ch. Row 2: Ch-3, 1-dc, repeat (ch-2, 2-dc in ch of previous row, ch-3, 2-dc). Row 3: Work same as for Row 2 at corners, make filter st with ch-2, 1-dc, on straight line. Work patterns as shown from Row 11. Work 5-dc puff on Rows 12 and 24. Work around with sl st-picot with 3-ch after dc and complete.

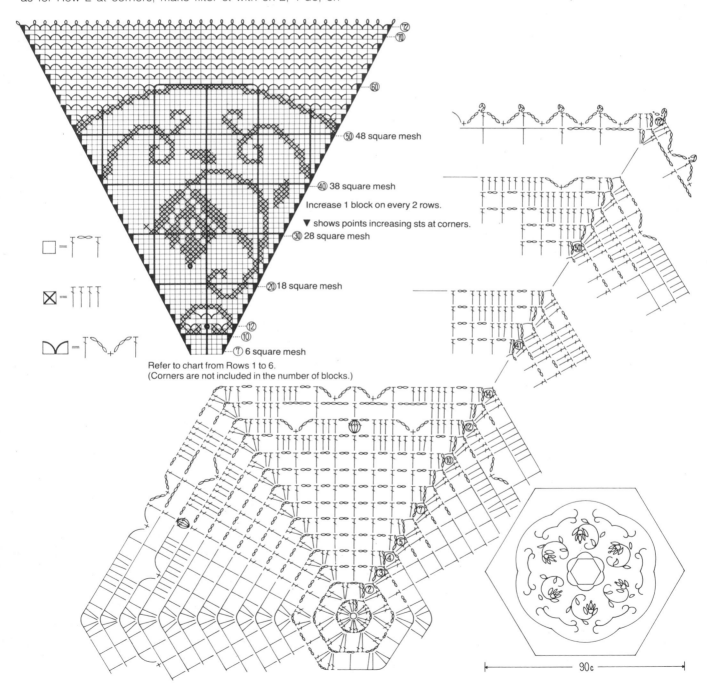

⑦ 6 square mesh
⑩
⑫
20 18 square mesh
30 28 square mesh
40 38 square mesh
50 48 square mesh
60
⑩
⑫

Increase 1 block on every 2 rows.

▼ shows points increasing sts at corners.

Refer to chart from Rows 1 to 6.
(Corners are not included in the number of blocks.)

□ = ⌐⌐⌐
⊠ = ⌐⌐⌐⌐
⋈ = ⌐⌐⌐

◄— 90c —►

73

50

Abstract Arrangement

(50) 90 cm in diameter.   Instructions on page 78.

2

You'll need: DMC crochet cotton No. 40. 15g white (5200).
Steel crochet hook: Crochet hook 0.9 mm.
Finished size: 27 cm in diameter
Instructions: Row 1: Ch-3 (work following rows in same manner), 23-dc in loop. Row 2: Repeat (ch-5, 1-dc). Row 3: Work (2-dc, ch-2, 2-dc, ch-3, 1-dc, ch-2, 1-dc, ch-3) around.

Work changing the number of ch from Rows 4 to 6. Make pineapple pattern between shell st from Rows 8 to 18, changing sts of ch. Work sl st-picot with 3-ch around on the last row.

27c

1

You'll need: DMC crochet cotton No. 30. 320 white (5200).

Steel crochet hook: Crochet hook 1.5 mm.

Finished size: 120 cm in diameter

Instructions: Ch-8, join with sl st to form ring. **Row 1:** 24-dc (include the beginning ch). **Row 2:** Repeat (1-dc, ch-1). **Row 3:** Work ch-2 between dc. **Row 4:** Work ch-3 between dc, 3-dc at every three blocks. This row is the base of 8 sections. Make pineapple patterns 2 times from Rows 5 to 31. Make pineapples at each section (32 in all) from Rows 49 to 81. Complete with sl st-picot with 5-ch on the last row.

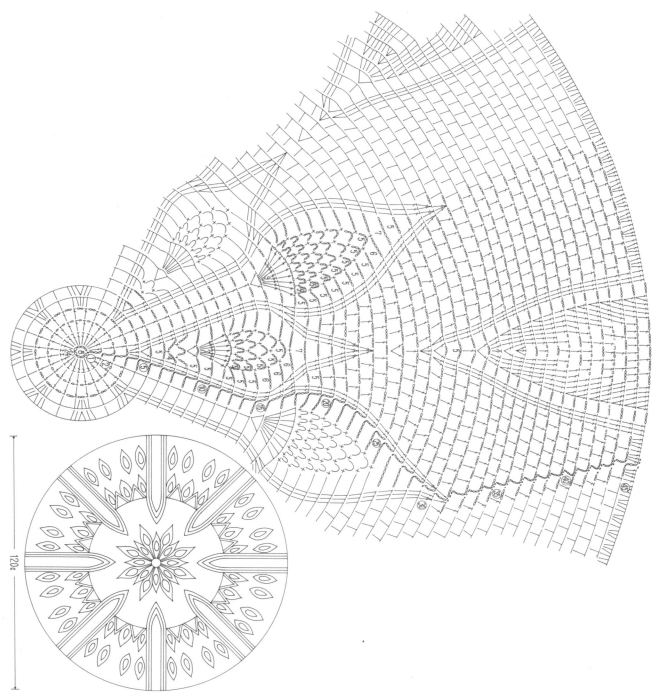

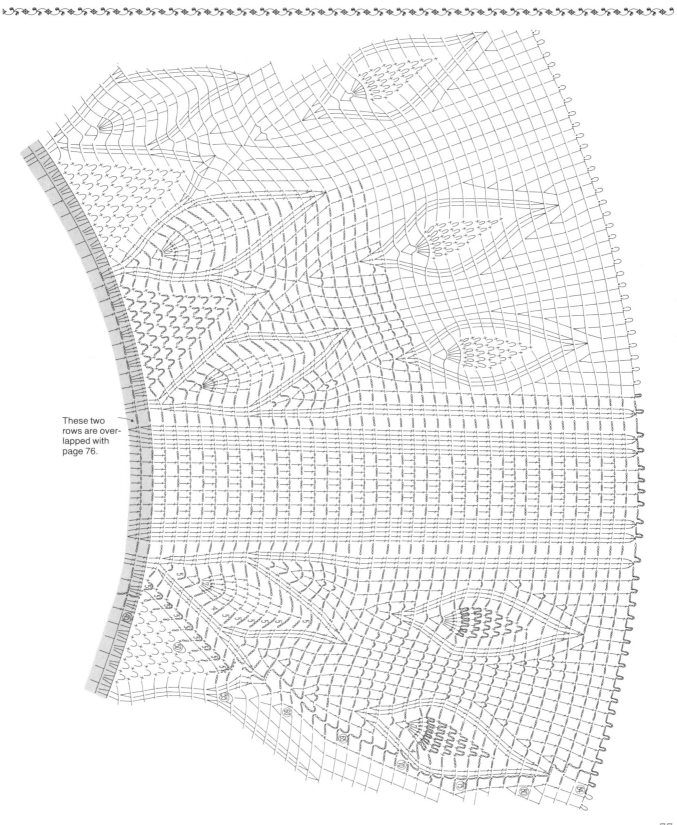

These two rows are over-lapped with page 76.

3

You'll need: DMC crochet cotton No. 40. 15g white (5200).
Steel crochet hook: Crochet hook 0.9 mm.
Finished size: 25 cm in diameter
Instructions: Row 1: Ch-3, 15-dc in ring. Row 2: Repeat (ch-5, skip 1 st, 1-dc). Row 3: Repeat ch-3, 5-dc. From Row 4, work in same manner, making pineapple patterns from Rows 7 to 16. Work 4-dc puff from Rows 20 to 22. Work around with sl st-picot with 3-ch on the last row.

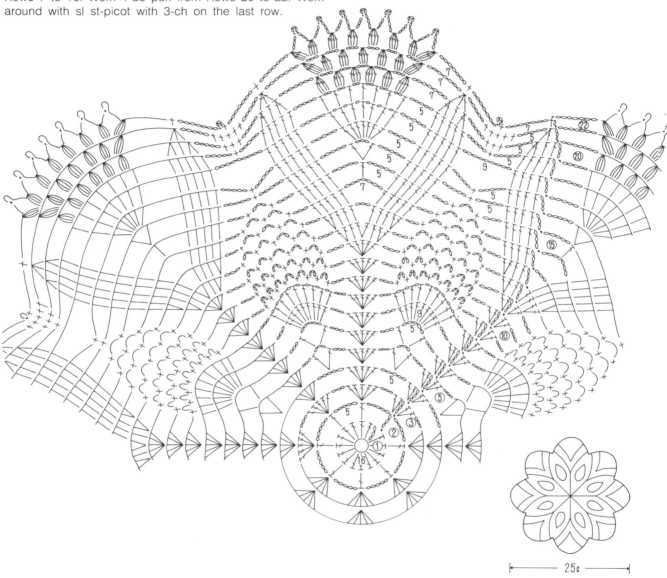

25c

You'll need: DMC crochet cotton No. 40. 15g white (5200).
Steel crochet hook: Crochet hook 0.9 mm.
Finished size: 29 cm in diameter
Instructions: Row 1: 12-sc in loop. **Row 2:** Ch-7 at the beginning, (ch-5, 1-quintuple tr) 11 times, ch-5. **Row 3:** Ch-3

at the beginning, ch-3, 1-dc and repeat (ch-5, 1-dc, ch-3, 1-dc in same st as previous dc). Make 6 sections from Row 4. Work 3-dc puff from Row 18. Work around with sl st-picot with 3-ch on the last row.

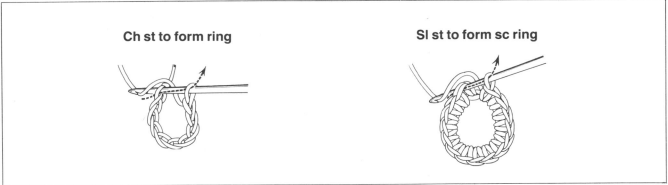

Ch st to form ring

Sl st to form sc ring

5

You'll need: DMC crochet cotton No. 40. 40g white (5200).
Steel crochet hook: Crochet hook 0.9 mm.
Finished size: 38 cm in diameter
Instructions: Row 1: Ch-3 at the beginning (ch-1, 1-dc) 15 times, ch-1 at the end of row. Row 2: Work ch-3 between dc. **Row 3:** Work 2-dc and 1-dc alternately in dc of previous row, ch-3 between dc. From Row 4, work increasing sts, taking notice of repetitions in pineapple patterns. Complete with 3-ch picot on the last row.

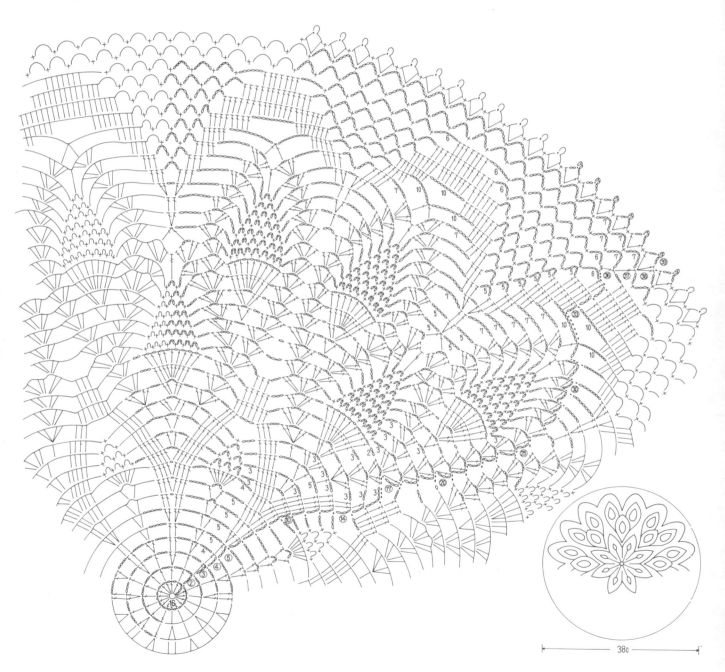

38c

You'll need: DMC crochet cotton No. 40. 35g white (5200).
Steel crochet hook: Crochet hook 0.9 mm.
Finished size: 33 cm in diameter
Instructions: Row 1: Ch-4 at the beginning, (ch-3, 1-tr) 11 times; join with ch-1 and 1-hdc to form ring. Row 2: Work

(ch-4, 1-sc) around. On Row 3, work ch-5 between sc. From Row 4, work referring to chart. On Row 28, sl st in loop of Row 26 from wrong side and continue to Row 29.

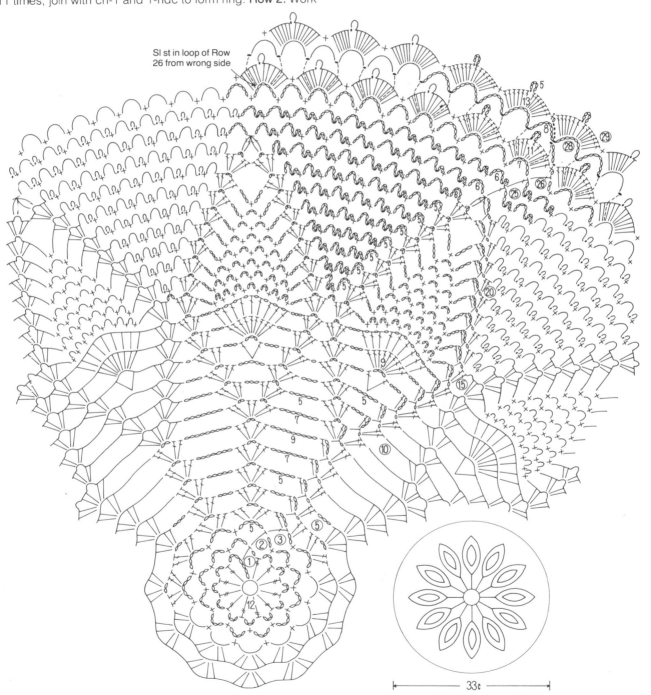

Sl st in loop of Row 26 from wrong side

33㎝

You'll need: DMC crochet cotton No. 40. 10g white (5200).
Steel crochet hook: Crochet hook 0.9 mm.
Finished size: 20 cm in diameter
Instructions: Row 1: Make a loop at the end of thread, work 24-tr (include the beginning ch). Row 2: Repeat (2-tr, ch-2). Row 3: Sl st in 2 sts of previous row, work around with

(2-tr, ch-2, 4-tr (note the point to pick up), ch-3, 2-tr). Work referring to chart from Row 4, making pineapple pattern from Rows 8 to 16 and 3-tr puff from Rows 14 to 18.

20c

You'll need: DMC crochet cotton No. 40. 10g white (5200).
Steel crochet hook: Crochet hook 0.9 mm.
Finished size: 24 cm in diameter
Instructions: Ch-8, join with sl st to form ring. **Row 1:** (2-dc (include the beginning ch), ch-1) 8 times. **Row 2:**

Repeat (2-dc, ch-1, 2-dc, ch-1) in ch of previous row. From Rows 3 to 16, make diamond pattern increasing and decreasing dc. Work 2-dc cluster on Rows 17 to 23 and 3-dc puff on Row 23. Work sl st in sts of previous row at the beginning of Rows 18, 22, and 24.

24c

You'll need: DMC crochet cotton No. 40. 10g white (5200).
Steel crochet hook: Crochet hook 0.9 mm.
Finished size: 21.5 cm in diameter
Instructions: Ch-8, join with sl st to form ring. **Row 1:** Ch-1 (1-sc, ch-10) 8 times, sl st in 5-ch of beginning. **Row 2:** Ch-3 (work following row in same manner), repeat (ch-3, 1-dc, ch-3, 1-dc). **Row 3:** Work shell st of 2-dc and ch, joining with sc. **Row 4:** Work shell st of 3-dc in same manner. From Row 5, work shell st of tr and make pineapple pattern from Row 6.

├──── 21.5c ────┤

You'll need: DMC crochet cotton No. 40. 10g white (5200).
Steel crochet hook: Crochet hook 0.9 mm.
Finished size: 20 cm in diameter
Instructions: Ch-8, join with sl st to form ring. **Row 1:** 16-sc. **Row 2:** Ch-4, 2-tr cluster, (ch-5, 3-tr puff) 7 times, ch-5. Work puff in same way until Row 5. On Row 6, repeat (17-sc, ch-5). After Row 7, work net st and tr. On Row 19, work tr puff and ch joining with sc and complete.

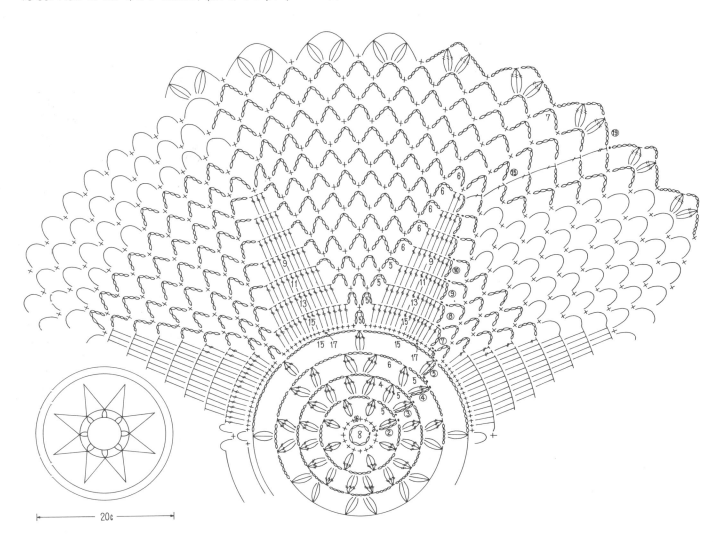

— 20c —

11

You'll need: DMC crochet cotton No. 40. 10g white (5200).
Steel crochet hook: Crochet hook 0.9 mm.
Finished size: 23 cm in diameter
Instructions: Row 1: Make a loop at end of thread, (1-tr (include the beginning ch) ch-3) 8 times. **Row 2:** Repeat (5-tr, ch-2) in ch of previous row. **Row 3:** Repeat (7-tr (pick up ch of previous row at both ends), ch-3). **Row 4:** Repeat (5-tr cluster, ch-4, 5-tr in ch of previous row, ch-4). Hereafter, work same pattern as for Rows 2 to 4, but join with tr, dtr, tr tr, quintuple tr and sextuple tr at the end of net st.

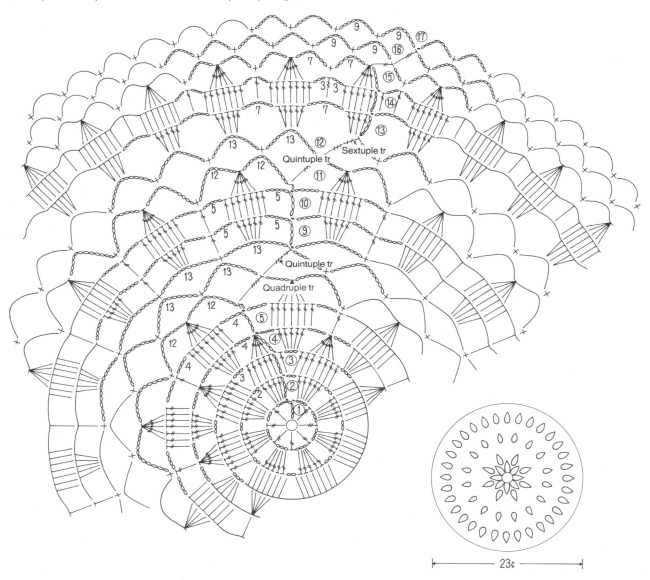

23c

You'll need: DMC crochet cotton No. 40. 10g white (5200).
Steel crochet hook: Crochet hook 0.9 mm.
Finished size: 17 cm in diameter
Instructions: Ch-6, join with sl st to form ring. **Row 1:** Ch-3, 15-dc. **Row 2:** Ch-4, 1-tr, and repeat (ch-3, 2-tr cluster). Continue, referring to chart. Work 3-tr puff on Row 5. Do not mix up 5-dc cluster, 4-dc puff, and 4-dc cluster on Row 20.

17c

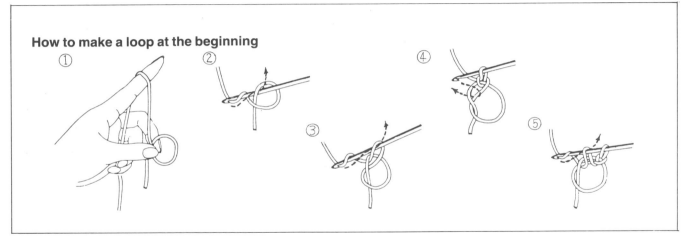

How to make a loop at the beginning

① ② ③ ④ ⑤

13

You'll need: DMC crochet cotton No. 40. 10g white (5200).
Steel crochet hook: Crochet hook 0.9 mm.
Finished size: 24 cm in diameter
Instructions: Row 1: 12-sc in loop, join with sl st to form ring. Row 2: (1-sc, ch-5) 5 times, ch-2, 1-dc at the end of row. Row 3: Repeat (ch-7, 1-sc, ch-2, sl st-picot with 3-ch, ch-2, 1-sc). Row 4: Sl st in 3 sts of previous row, work (7-dc (include the beginning ch-3), ch-5) around. Work 3-dc puff from Rows 6 to 10. Finish working sl st-picot with 3-ch on the last row.

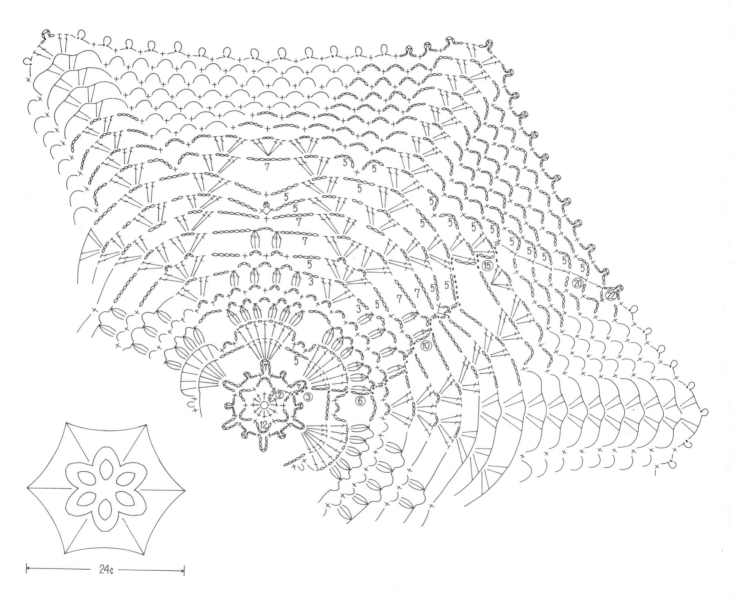

24c

88

14

You'll need: DMC crochet cotton No. 40. 10g cream (745).
Steel crochet hook: Crochet hook 0.9 mm.
Finished size: 17 cm×17 cm
Instructions: Row 1: Make a loop at the end of thread, (2-dc (include the beginning ch-3), ch-5) 4 times. **Row 2:**

Work 6-dc between ch-5. **Row 3:** Sl st in 2 sts of previous row, repeat (4-dc, ch-5). Continue in same manner except changing the number of ch and dc. Work sl st-picot with 3-ch on the last row.

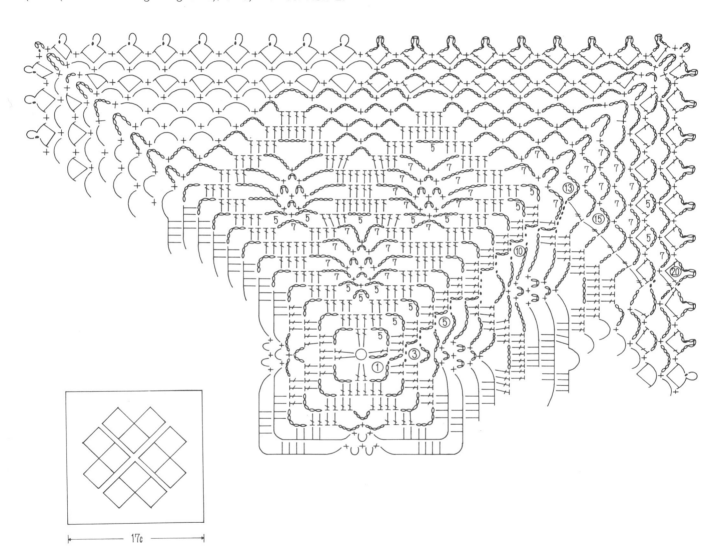

17c

You'll need: DMC crochet cotton No. 40. 10g white (5200).
Steel crochet hook: Crochet hook 0.9 mm.
Finished size: 22 cm in diameter
Instructions: Row 1: Make a loop at the end of thread, ch-3, (ch-3, 1-dc) 7 times, ch-1 1-hdc. Row 2: Repeat (ch-5, 1-sc), ch-2, 1-dc at the end of row. Row 3: Ch-3 (work following row in same manner), 2-dc, repeat (ch-5, 3-dc),

noting sts to pick up. Continue in same way, working sl st in 3 sts of previous row at the beginning. Work around sl st-picot with 3-ch and ch-picot alternately on the last row.

Quintuple tr

22c

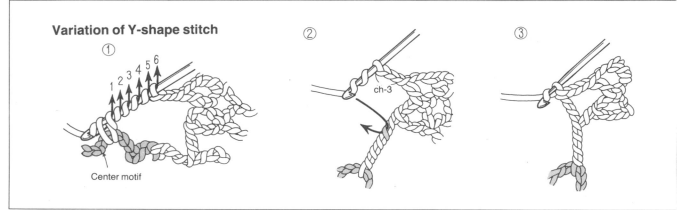

Variation of Y-shape stitch

① 1 2 3 4 5 6

Center motif

② ch-3

③

You'll need: DMC crochet cotton No. 40. 10g pink (818).
Steel crochet hook: Crochet hook 0.9 mm.
Finished size: 20cm in diameter
Instructions: Row 1: Make a loop at the end of thread, ch-1, 16-sc. Row 2: Work around with (1-dc, ch-3), ch-1, 1-hdc at the end. (Work following row in same manner.) Row 3: Repeat (ch-5, 1-sc). Row 4: Repeat (3-tr puff, ch-7). Row 5: Work net st of ch-7. Row 6: Work around with (1-dc, ch-8, variation of dc in 1st st of ch-8, 1-dc, ch-1, 1-sc, sl st-picot

with 3-ch, 1-sc, ch-1). Continue to Row 7, working sl st at the end of row. Work net st and puff from Rows 7 to 16. Work Row 17 the same as Row 6. Complete with shell st of 9-dc and ch-picot around on Row 18.

|← 20c →|

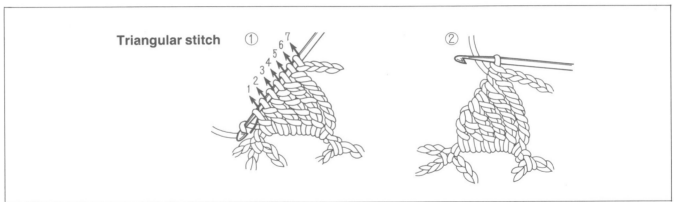

Triangular stitch

You'll need: DMC crochet cotton No. 40. 10g white (5200).
Steel crochet hook: Crochet hook 0.9 mm.
Finished size: 19.5 cm in diameter
Instructions: Row 1: Make a loop at the end of thread, 16-sc. **Row 2:** Ch-3 at the beginning of the row (work following row in same manner), repeat (ch-5, 2-dc cluster (scoop every other sc of previous row)). **Row 3:** Repeat 1-sc, ch-5. **Row 4:** Work (2-dc, ch-3, 2-dc, ch-1 1-sc, sl st-picot with 3-ch, 1-sc, ch-1). Work following, changing the number of sts and complete with sl st-picot with 3-ch on Row 17.

16-sc

19.5c

22·23

You'll need: DMC crochet cotton No. 40. 22 = 10g white (5200). Crochet cotton No. 40. 23 = 30g gradation of green, light purple, yellow, blue, and pink.
Steel crochet hook: Crochet hook 0.9 mm.
Finished size: 22 = 21 cm in diameter. 23 = 39 cm in diameter
Instructions: The instructions for making 22 and 23 are the same. Make a loop at the end of thread. **Row 1:** (2-dc

(include the beginning ch-3), ch-3) 12 times. **Row 2:** Sl st in 2 sts of previous row, repeat (2-dc, ch-4, 2-dc). From Row 3, increase the numbers of ch and dc. When the number of ch becomes a lot, work sextuple tr and ninefold tr to continue on next row. Work to Row 8 on doily 22, and continue working to Row 12 on doily 23 to complete.

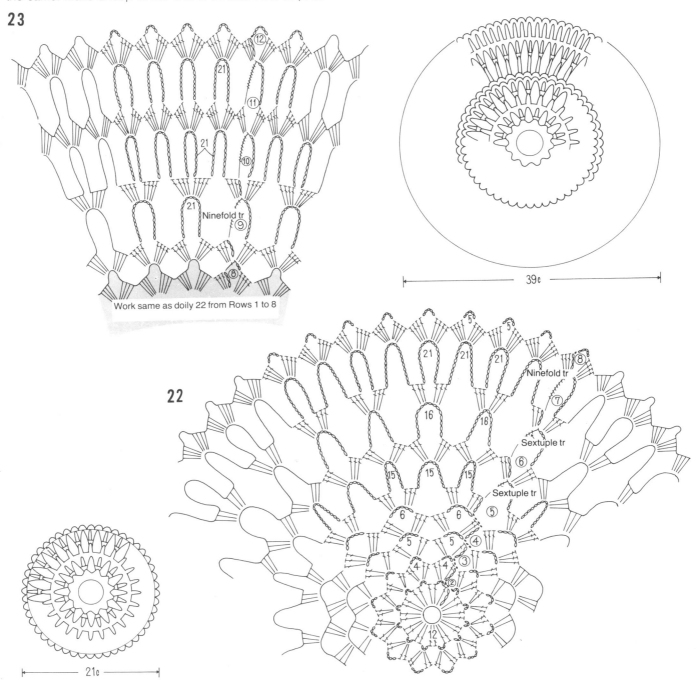

23

Work same as doily 22 from Rows 1 to 8

39c

22

Ninefold tr

Sextuple tr

Sextuple tr

21c

You'll need: DMC crochet cotton No. 40. 10g each of light yellow (744) and blue (519).

Steel crochet hook: Crochet hook 1.0 mm.

Finished size: 28 cm in diameter

Instructions: Row 1: Make a loop with blue, ch-4 at the beginning, 24-tr. Row 2: Use light yellow, repeating (ch-1, 1-tr) around. Rows 3–12: Work with blue on odd rows and light yellow on even rows, putting light yellow over blue. Use blue on Rows 14 and 15 and light yellow on Rows 16 and 17. Work with blue on Row 18 and light yellow on Row 19 to complete.

Color	Row
blue	①③⑤⑦⑨⑪⑭⑮⑱
light yellow	②④⑥⑧⑩⑫⑬⑯⑰⑲

32

Shown on page 35

You'll need: DMC crochet cotton No. 40. Some yellow green (954), green (913), yellow (743), dark pink (776), blue (798), crimson (321), and orange (740).

Steel crochet hook: Crochet hook 0.9 mm.

Finished size: 27 cm in diameter

Instructions: Work in accordance with color chart. Ch-12, join with sl st to form ring. **Row 1:** 24-sc. **Row 2:** (1-tr (include the beginning ch), ch-6) 8 times. **Row 3:** Repeat (2-sl st-picot with 7-ch, 7-sc). Work following rows the same

as Rows 2 and 3, changing colors. **Row 18:** Repeat around with (ch-8, triple tr, 1-dtr, ch-1, 1-tr, (ch-10, 5-sl st) 2 times, 1-tr, ch-1, 1-dtr, ch-1, triple tr, ch-8, sl st, (2-sc, sl st-picot with 3-ch) 2 times, 1-sc, sl st), and break off.

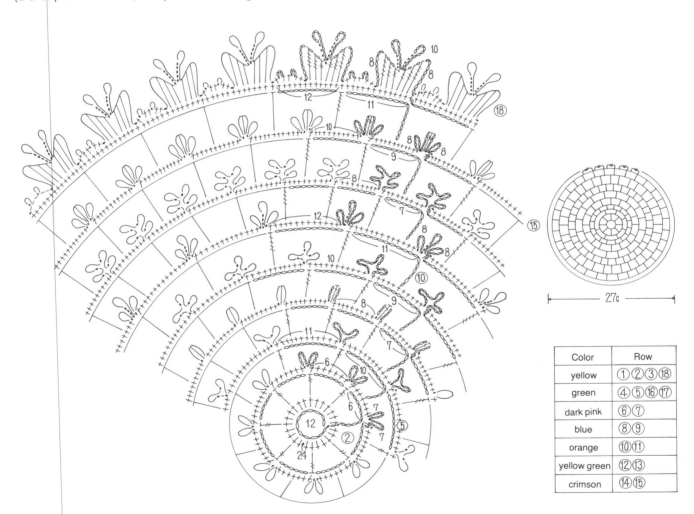

Color	Row
yellow	① ② ③ ⑱
green	④ ⑤ ⑯ ⑰
dark pink	⑥ ⑦
blue	⑧ ⑨
orange	⑩ ⑪
yellow green	⑫ ⑬
crimson	⑭ ⑮

Basics of Crochet Stitches and Symbols

○ Chain stitch (ch)	①	②	③	④

● Slip stitch (sl st)	①	②

✚ Single crochet (sc)	①	②	③

⊤ Half double crochet (hdc)	① Wind thread once. First ch-2	②	③

⊤ Double crochet (dc)	① Wind thread once. First ch-3	② (a)	③ (b)	④

⊤ Treble crochet (tr)	① Wind thread twice. First ch-4	② (a)	③ (b)	④	⑤ (c)

Double treble crochet (dtr) ⫘

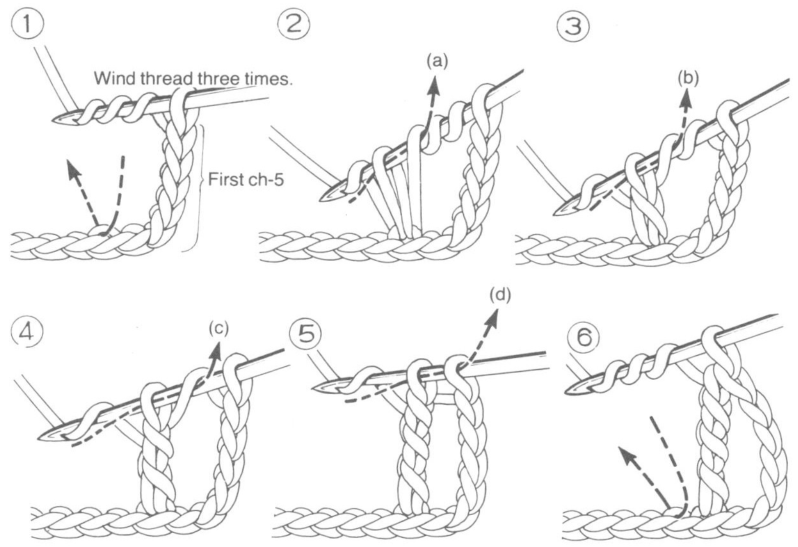

① Wind thread three times.

First ch-5

② (a)

③ (b)

④ (c)

⑤ (d)

⑥

Variation of sc ✛|

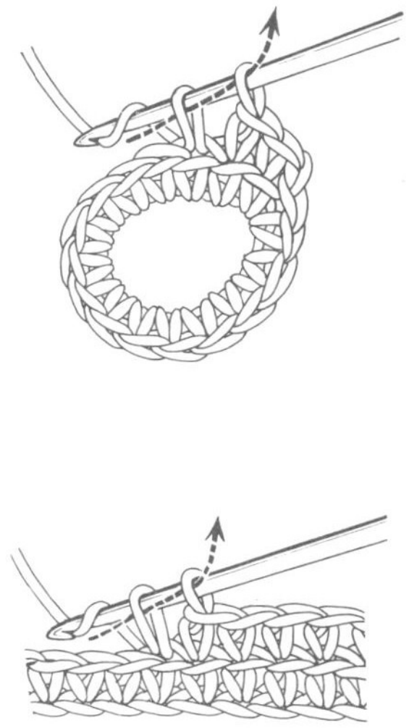

2-double-crochet cluster (2-dc cluster) ⅄

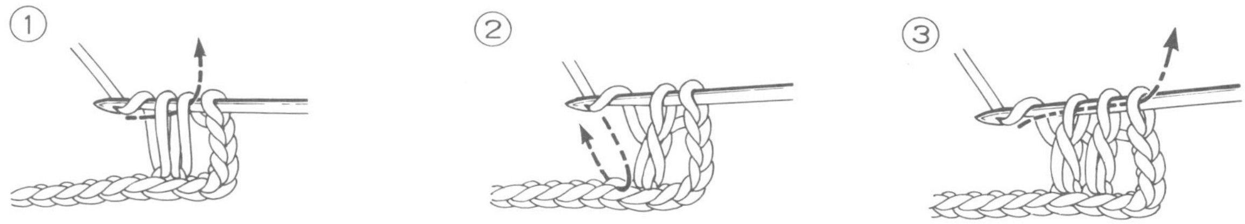

① ② ③

3-double-crochet puff (3-dc puff) ⊕

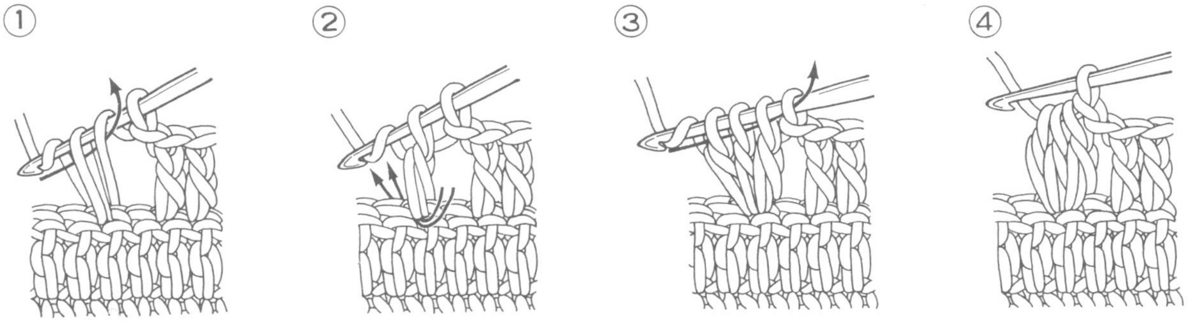

① ② ③ ④

5-double-crochet popcorn (5-dc pop.) ⊕

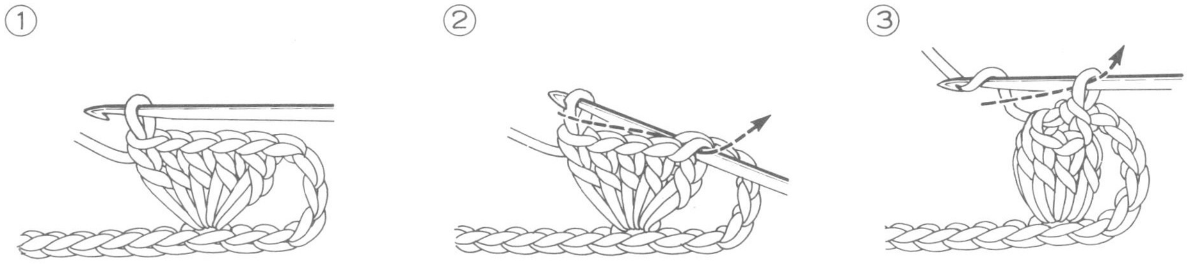

① ② ③

97

Finishing

It is said that good crochet work depends on the way it is finished. This step is very important, because orderly stitches are the basis of a beautiful pattern. You will have excellent results with your finished crochet lace if you keep these points in midn.

Before finishing, check:
① the treatment of cotton ends before and after working ② the treatment of cotton ends connected or joined during the work ③ for stains or spots on lace.

Tools required for finishing:
① Ironing board—soft and well padded to protect stitches. ② Iron. ③ Towel. ④ Covering cloth—both 3 and 4 should be plain white. ⑤ A neutral detergent. ⑥ Spray starch. ⑦ Water sprayer. ⑧ Rustproof finishing pins. ⑨ Finishing board—e.g., sulfate paper.

Finished size
The sizes given in the directions are those after finishing. In other words, the crocheted size is smaller than the finished size.

How to draw guidelines

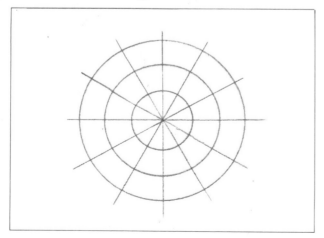

In the case of a circle, draw the circle to the finished size. Then draw division lines according to the size of the pattern. (Draw with a fine-line pen or a pencil.) When using a pencil,

98

iron on the drawing to avoid a rise of lead. In the case of other shapes, draw lines according to the work, and follow the same procedure as for the circle.

How to pin

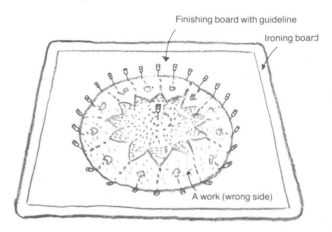

Turn your work over on a board. Pin it at the center first, then at appropriate places according to the guidelines and the stretching capacity of the crochet. Increase the number of pins gradually. When a piece is well stretched, remove the pin at the center before ironing.

How to iron

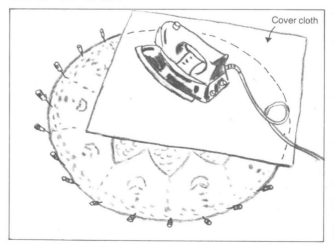

After water is sprayed all over the crochet, spray on starch, and iron it, very hot, over a covering cloth. Be careful not to burn the crochet. After it has dried completely, remove pins. (Stains or spots on lace should be washed out beforehand.)